Beginner's Guide to
Feltmaking

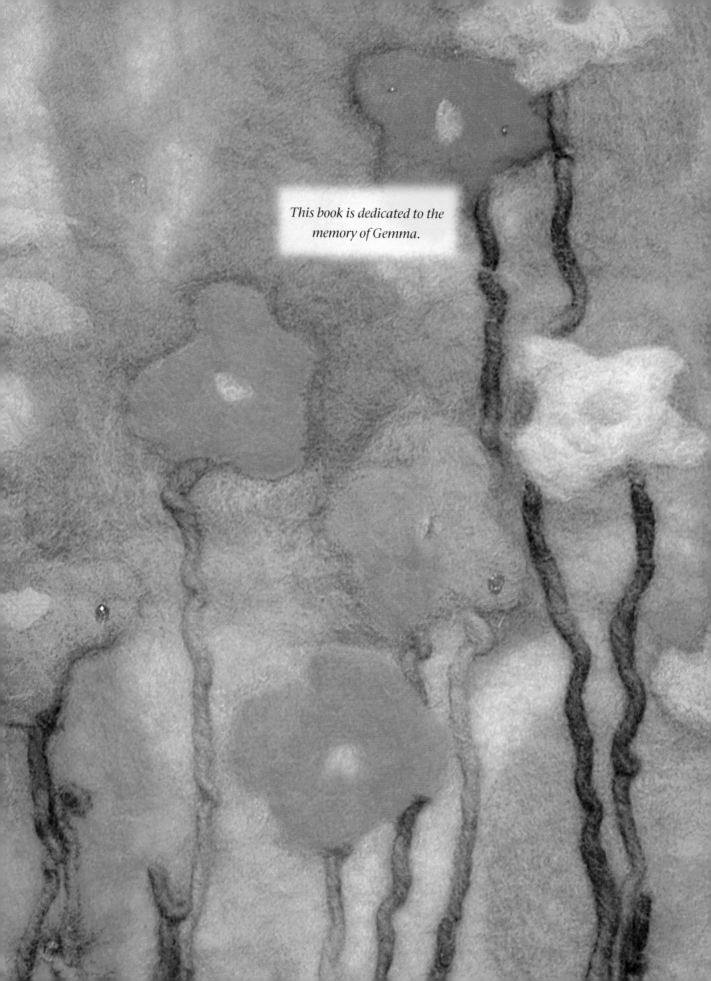

This book is dedicated to the memory of Gemma.

Beginner's Guide to
Feltmaking

SHIRLEY ASCHER AND JANE BATEMAN

SEARCH PRESS

First published in Great Britain 2006

Search Press Limited
Wellwood, North Farm Road,
Tunbridge Wells, Kent TN2 3DR

Reprinted 2006, 2007

Text copyright © Shirley Ascher and Jane Bateman 2006

Photographs by Charlotte de la Bédoyère, Search Press Studios,
Roddie Paine Photographic Studios and Mike Ritchie (inside
front cover)

Photographs and design copyright © Search Press Ltd 2006

ISBN 10: 1-84448- 004- 6
ISBN 13: 978-184448-004-3

The Publishers and authors can accept no responsibility for any
consequences arising from the information, advice or instructions
given in this publication.

Suppliers
If you have difficulty in obtaining any of the materials and
equipment mentioned in this book, please visit the Search Press
website for details of suppliers: www.searchpress.com

Alternatively, you can write to the Publishers at the address above,
for a current list of stockists, including firms which operate a mail-
order service.

Publishers' note

All the step-by-step photographs in this book feature
the authors, Shirley Ascher and Jane Bateman,
demonstrating feltmaking techniques. No models have
been used.

Acknowledgements

*Thanks to the British Museum who provided us with
information about the origins of felt. Also, thanks
to Janet and Peter Garner at Morden Hall Alpacas,
Hertfordshire who gave us the opportunity to give our
first feltmaking demonstration; Rita Peace, also in
Hertfordshire, for introducing us to her flock of rare-
breed North Ronaldsay and Hebridean sheep and
giving us some fleece to experiment with; and Candia
Midworth, British Camelids Ltd, for allowing us to
use her photograph of alpacas on page 56.*

*We would also like to thank the following suppliers
for their sponsorship and support: The Handweavers
Studio and Gallery Ltd, Walthamstow; Art Van Go,
Stevenage; and Wingham Wool Works,
South Yorkshire.*

*And finally, with special thanks to both our families
for all their support.*

*Front cover: Detail from the waterlilies wallhanging (see page 41).
The insets (from left to right) are taken from the sheep project
(page 52), the lollipop flowers project (page 68) and the paintbox
project (page 72); the fourth inset shows a variation based on the
meadow design (see page 37).*

*Back cover: These three images are taken from the meadow
project (see page 32).*

*Page 1: Detail from a pincushion based on
the poppies design (see page 29).*

*Page 3: Alpaca wallhanging. The alpaca and
flower shapes were cut from half-felt and inlaid on
to the background fibres (see page 56).*

*Page 5: Waterlilies wallhanging. Instructions
for making a similar piece are provided on
pages 38–41.*

Contents

Introduction

Feltmaking has a rich history that goes back thousands of years. From earliest times this versatile fabric has been used in many different cultures, from the nomads of Asia and Mongolia, to the warriors of China and the soldiers of Rome. Evidence of felt has been found in Turkish wall paintings dating back to 6500 BC, and in Scandinavia felt is believed to have been around since the Iron Age. Hard-wearing, durable and warm, throughout history it has been used to make carpets, blankets, tent coverings, boots, hats and much more. It is still made and used today in many countries where conditions are harsh. There is also a revival of interest amongst crafters who are rediscovering the joys of working with a textile that can be worked flat, moulded, used three dimensionally and embellished with embroidery, appliqué and beads. It has a unique appeal, the techniques are easy and there are endless possibilities for artistic expression.

Unspun wool fibres are used in the feltmaking process. Each strand is covered in tiny scales, and when water and pressure are applied, the fibres open up and tangle together to form a dense fabric. Only hot water and soap flakes are required, and the results are amazing. You can create anything from sumptuous wallhangings and stylish cushions to shaped and sculpted items – all from a kitchen-sink studio. The fabric is user friendly, wonderfully soft and a pleasure to work with. One of its most useful qualities is that it does not fray, so cut edges need not be finished off and nothing is ever wasted. Even the smallest scraps can be used for appliqué work, or made into items such as greetings cards or pincushions.

Feltmaking has taken us down many avenues on a fascinating journey of discovery, from the British Museum to numerous art and craft exhibitions, and even to an alpaca farm to seek out alternative materials. At every turn we have been greeted with enthusiasm. This book has been inspired by the positive reaction of all those who have seen our work and who have encouraged us along the way. We have included a whole range of projects, from a simple square that can be framed, or made into a place mat or a cushion, through to stunning wallhangings, tea cosies and felted stones. Once you have become familiar with the basic techniques, you can start creating your own designs. We hope your experiences with this amazing fabric will be as enjoyable as ours have been.

Jane

Shirley

Opposite
Flowers

This wallhanging was inspired by a painting by the French artist Odilon Redon. The flower shapes and pot were cut from half-felt and laid on a bed of rich, dark purple fibres. Silks were added to some of the massed flowers and to the pot to make them shine out against the background.

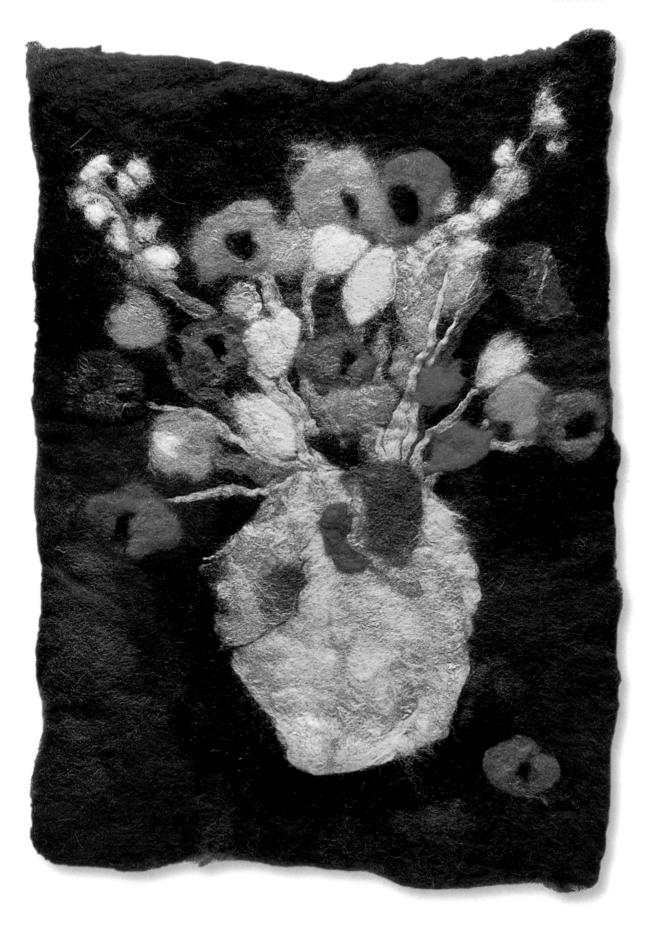

Materials and equipment

People are often pleasantly surprised by the simplicity of feltmaking. You do not need any specialised equipment, apart from the fibres and embellishments. The whole process can be carried out at the kitchen sink or on a table in the garden, and all you need are a few household items.

Fibres

All kinds of animal wool, hair and fur can be felted, some more successfully than others. We prefer to use prepared sheep's fleece but you can also use mohair, cashmere, alpaca and fibres from the llama, camel, goat, yak and possum. The International Feltmaker's Association is keen to encourage feltmakers throughout the world to use locally produced fibres, so it is worthwhile seeking a source in your area.

Natural and synthetic fibres, such as silk, ramie and dip-dyed yarns, can be incorporated into feltmaking. They have to be mixed with the basic fibre, or wisped over (see page 25) to ensure that they are felted into the finished piece. Look out for interesting textured yarns. You may find something special to embellish a wallhanging, panel or cushion.

Natural and synthetic fibres such as silk, dip-dyed yarns, ramie and textured yarns can be incorporated when the wool fibres are being laid out. Brightly coloured beads can be stitched into the finished piece.

Embellishments

Finished pieces can be embellished with beads, buttons and shells – whatever you fancy. Appliquéd felt motifs can also be added to enhance texture and colour. Also, reconsider other pieces of felt you have made that you are not quite happy with. We often recycle them by cutting out shapes of flowers, leaves, etc. to add to our latest creation.

Our favourite fibres to work with are dyed merino combed tops. They are available in a wide selection of gorgeous colours. We have used them in all the projects in this book, apart from the alpaca project, though other fibres mentioned could be used instead.

Types of wool

There are many different types of wool and you should try as many as you can to help you decide which ones you prefer to use. Before it can be used, raw fleece has to be cleaned and carded to smooth out any tangled fibres and to remove dirt (see page 24). Prepared fibres are either carded (a mass of loose fibres) or they are 'combed tops' (a long, soft rope of parallel fibres).

We prefer to use prepared sheep's wool and usually work with merino combed tops, which are quick to felt and wonderfully soft. We also like the wools from Wensleydale and Falkland sheep, though they are slightly hairier than merino and therefore the felt is not so soft.

Here we have included the most popular wools. Some of their fibres are softer than others, but all of them will felt beautifully. There are several factors that will affect the quality of a finished piece: the thickness and length of the fibre, which animal it comes from, the lustre ('sheen') and the crimp ('waviness'). All these qualities will affect the look and feel of the finished piece of felt.

Black Welsh

Long, even, chocolate brown fibres, not quite as soft as merino but very quick and easy to felt. A pleasure to work with.

Falkland

These lovely soft fibres make a nice firm felt.

Cheviot Light Grey

These are quite coarse fibres that make a loose, hairy felt.

Jacob Humbug

These fibres are fairly coarse, but, as the name suggests, give an interesting stripey effect.

 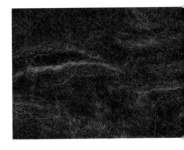

Shetland Humbug

Soft and easier to felt than the Jacob Humbug. The cream streaks give an interesting humbug effect.

Merino

This is the best felter. It is the most commonly used wool for felting and is widely available. It is our personal favourite and we use it in most of the projects in this book.

Herdwick Light Grey

These short, coarse fibres are slow to felt and the texture of the felt is slightly wiry.

Dorset Horn

This is a good felter, with a soft, slightly hairy finish.

Wensleydale curls

These gorgeous curls can be combined with merino fibres to create exciting, textured felt. Wensleydale is also available uncarded and as combed tops.

North Ronaldsay

This fleece is from a rare breed of sheep known as North Ronaldsay. The fibres are fairly soft and fluffy and a bit slow to mesh, but they make a firm and solid felt.

Equipment

The felting method that we recommend uses calico to contain the prepared fibres, and bubble wrap to create friction. Another method uses netting and bamboo mats to roll the fibres and achieve a denser result by 'fulling' the felt. The calico/bubble wrap method can be less messy, especially if you use a large plastic tray to contain the felt and water. The finished felt is softer and particularly suitable for wallhangings.

For all the projects in this book we use medium-weight, pre-washed **calico** or **cotton cloth** to wrap the prepared fibres in.

A large shallow **plastic tray** is used during the wet stage of felting. The type used under a garden growing bag works well.

You will need a **shallow dish** with a flat bottom to make 'saucer' felt.

Bubble wrap is used to create friction to speed up the felting process. It can also be cut and used as a resist material for making shaped items.

To prepare the fibres, you will need **hand carders** or **pet combs** with wire teeth.

Soap flakes speed up the felting by improving the elasticity of the fibres and making a slippery surface that is easier to rub.

A **kettle** is useful to heat water. We use water just off the boil, but warm water can be used if you are working with children.

Use a **jug** to hold the hot water and a **balloon whisk** to mix in the soap flakes. You can also sprinkle soap flakes directly on to the fibres.

It is advisable to protect your hands with **rubber gloves** when using hot water.

A few drops of **vinegar** can be added to the final rinse to remove the last traces of soap.

A plastic **plant sprayer** is useful for dampening the fibres when you are making shaped items.

You will need small, sharp **scissors** to cut out half-felt shapes and larger ones for other tasks.

A **soft pencil** and a **ruler** are used to mark out the area on the calico on which to lay out the fibres.

You will need a **tape measure** to check dimensions, **dressmaking pins** to pin the calico and a **needle and thread** to secure the prepared fibres in the calico.

The felt is rolled up in a **towel** to remove excess moisture before pressing the felt with an **iron**.

Optional items

A **cutting board** and **rotary cutter** are useful for trimming the edges of your felt.

A **kitchen timer** helps to keep track of time during the wet stage of felting, particularly when half-felts are being made, as these can become unworkable if they are rubbed for too long.

All of the equipment that you need for feltmaking is shown in the picture above.

Colour

Prepared wool fibres for feltmaking are available in a fantastic array of colours that can be mixed together or used as they are, but in order to do this effectively it helps if you know a little about the science of colour mixing and balancing.

When making felt, we find that bright and vibrant colours work well for wallhangings and cushions. However, stunning results can also be achieved using natural undyed fibres (see the items on page 59, which use natural shades of alpaca fibres).

Colour wheel

The colour wheel – the acknowledged tool of artists and designers – is useful in deciding which colours go well together, and which clash.

A simple colour wheel is made up of six colours: the three primary colours red, blue and yellow, and the three secondary colours orange, green and violet.

The secondary colours sit between the primaries and are made of fifty per cent of each of the two colours on either side. The third, or tertiary, colours are hues that lie between the primary and secondary colours. Again, they are the mid-point between the colours that are on either side of them.

How do you decide which colours 'go together'? The following basic rules can help.

Complementary colours

These are the contrasting colours that lie directly opposite each other on the colour wheel: red and green, yellow and violet, and blue and orange. They are the strongest possible opposite colours, and it is a matter of personal preference whether together you find them joyful and uplifting, or jarring and unpleasant.

Harmonious colours

You may prefer the more gentle tones of the harmonious colours, the shades either side of the selected colour. They work together in a more gentle and undemanding way.

Tones

In a toning scheme, colours are selected from just one segment of the wheel, i.e. the blue/violets or orange/reds. These colours usually sit comfortably together.

Highlights

Finally, do not forget to use highlight or accent colours – the small, bright touches of toning or harmonious colour that will give the piece extra energy.

It is important that you know how to apply these rules when you first start working with colour, but when you feel more confident, don't be afraid to experiment!

Murray Squares

This wallhanging was inspired by a friend's colourful business card. The interesting juxtaposition of colours was achieved by placing together colours that are either harmonious, tonal or complementary. For example, orange and yellow (harmonious), green and blue (toning), and turquoise and orange (complementary). We made this piece using the applied felt method (see page 74). It is large enough to be hung against a window, and with the light shining through it resembles stained glass.

Making a start

Making felt is a simple process. All you need are wool fibres, hot water, soap flakes and friction. When hot water and pressure are applied to wool fibres, the fibres open up and tangle together to form a dense fabric. Soap flakes help speed up the process by changing the pH balance and improving the elasticity of the fibres. Bubble wrap creates friction, which also encourages the fibres to felt together.

Here we show how to make a simple piece of felt using merino combed tops in cream and two shades of orange. The fibres are laid out on a piece of calico that is a little over twice the width of the piece of felt you wish to make, and slightly deeper. The fabric is then flapped over to contain the fibres during the wet stage of felting.

Here are two possible designs for you to make. For those of you who may have difficulty with the squares design (it can be hard to line up the squares neatly), an alternative design is shown on page 23 that is easier to achieve but which uses the same techniques as the squares design.

You will need

Washed calico, approximately 70 x 35cm (28 x 14in)

Merino combed tops in cream, pale orange and bright orange (or colours of your choice)

2B pencil

Metal ruler

Scissors

Dressmaking pins

Needle and thread

Rubber gloves

Shallow plastic tray, large enough to contain a 28cm (11in) square of felt

Bubble wrap

Jug, soap flakes and hot water

Vinegar

Towel

Iron

Cutting mat and rotary cutter

1. Draw a 28cm (11in) square on the calico. The square should be drawn to the right of the centre of the fabric so there is enough fabric to flap over when you have laid out the fibres.

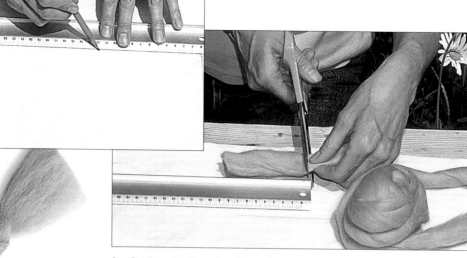

2. Cut 8cm (4in) lengths of the pale orange wool. You will need about eight to create the first layer of fibres. Some people prefer to pull off chunks rather than use scissors so that the ends of the fibres are less blunt.

3. To make the first layer, place a line of fibres on the calico. They should be vertical, with all the fibres facing towards you.

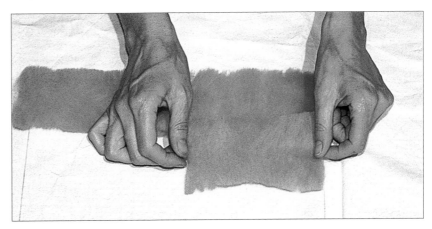

4. Lay down the second line of fibres so that they overlap the first line by approximately 1 cm (½in).

5. Continue placing lines of fibres in the same way until you have completed the first layer. If there are any gaps, fill them in with more fibres so the area marked out on the calico is completely covered.

6. Cut lengths of cream fibre and add a second layer, this time with the fibres running horizontally, from left to right.

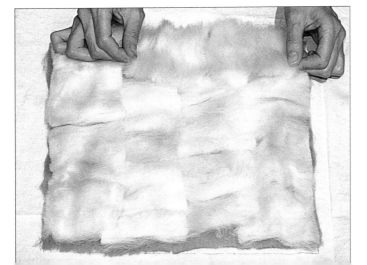

7. Start adding a third layer of cream fibres, again running at right angles to the previous layer.

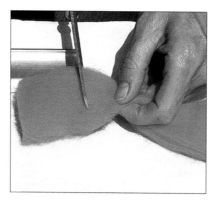

8. Complete the third layer. When the piece is felted, the bottom layer of fibres (pale orange) will show through the cream slightly to give the piece an orange hue. You are now ready to add your design.

9. For the squares design, cut three lengths from the bright orange fibre, each 5cm (2in) long.

10. Divide each length into two equal pieces and adjust them until they are roughly square. Repeat with the pale orange fibre. You will need nine squares in total for this design – five bright orange and four pale orange.

11. Place the squares on the bed of fibres, alternating bright and pale orange and keeping them fairly evenly spaced.

Tip

Use a 5cm (2in) square reverse template to help position your squares.

12. Fold the calico gently over the wool fibres. Keeping close to the edge of the sandwiched fibres, work round, carefully pinning the calico layers together.

13. Tack all round the edges and across the centre, then lay the calico parcel on a sheet of bubble wrap in a large shallow plastic tray.

Tip

The sheet of bubble wrap should be slightly deeper than the calico parcel, and just over twice the width so that it can be folded over to cover both sides of the calico.

The wet stage

14. Wearing a pair of rubber gloves to protect your hands, carefully pour hot water all over the sandwiched fibres.

15. Use a pressing action on the fibres for a few minutes until they are thoroughly soaked and settled.

16. Sprinkle on some soap flakes.

17. Press the soap flakes into the wet parcel to settle them. Add a little more hot water if there are any dry areas and to help dissolve the soap flakes.

18. Cover the parcel with bubble wrap and add a little more hot water and a few soap flakes to make a slippery surface.

19. Start to rub the felt parcel, gently at first and using a circular motion. Continue to rub for about fifteen minutes, turning the whole thing over half way through to work on the other side. You can increase the pressure as the fibres start to lock together.

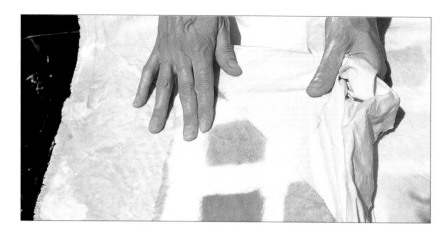

20. Check that the fibres have felted by unpicking the tacking stitches and peeling back some of the calico from one corner. The fibres should be starting to stick to the calico, but if they are still loose continue to rub the felt for five or ten minutes more.

21. Turn the parcel over and peel back the calico from the reverse side first to check there are no loose areas (this is a little like removing a sticking plaster). Do this before looking at the patterned side of the felted piece.

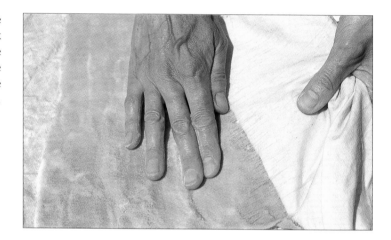

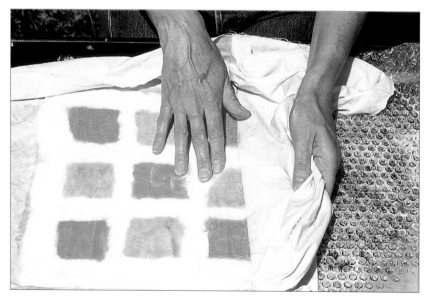

22. Remove the calico from the patterned side. The felt will be full of soap suds, which now have to be squeezed out and washed away.

23. Roll up the felt and squeeze out the excess suds.

24. Rinse the piece well until the water runs clear. Add a few drops of vinegar to the final rinse.

25. Remove the felt from the water and place it on a dry towel. Roll up the two layers together. The towel will absorb some of the water as the felt is squeezed between the layers.

26. Unroll the two layers, then gently press the felt with a fairly hot iron.

27. Place the felt on a cutting mat and trim the edges with a rotary cutter.

Tip

To firm up the felt you can put it through a machine wash cycle. Lay your piece of felt flat inside a pillowcase and tack to secure it. We find a 40°C short spin cycle works well (be prepared for shrinkage!), but washing machines vary so do some test runs before risking your favourite piece.

The finished panel

The finished panel can be used to make a cushion or a mat. If you are not sure about what colours to use, remember to keep it simple by choosing harmonious or toning schemes. Two shades of the same colour against a cream background look very effective.

A simple cushion can be made by joining together two pieces of felt by oversewing the edges with wool. We've used bobbles and stripes in two different shades of orange to create this simple, bold design.

Tip

To make bobbles, pull off a 20cm (8in) length of merino, wrap it round your finger and tuck in the end. Place it on a bed of fibres, pushing it down a little to help it felt in. Any bobbles that are still loose after felting can be secured with a stitch.

Bits and Pieces design

Divide 5 cm (2in) lengths of orange fibre into four pieces lengthways and make a diagonal cut at each end. Place alternate pale and bright orange pieces on the bed of fibres.

The finished panel.

To create this cushion, the felt panel has been trimmed and then sewn on to a piece of medium-weight cotton fabric. The same fabric has been used to make the back of the cushion, which has an envelope-style opening.

Carding

If you are using raw fleece it must be cleaned and carded to remove dirt and debris before it can be felted. Carding combs, or carders, are used to comb out the fleece so that the fibres are straightened and separated, and all run in the same direction.

Carding is not essential if you are using combed tops or fibres that have been pre-carded – these can simply be teased out by hand before being arranged in layers, as on pages 16–17.

Carders can also be used to mix different colours, and to organise the fibres so that they lie in fine and even layers and don't create lumps in the finished felt. Carders are also useful for brushing off any stray fibres from the calico prior to felting, and for removing any fibres that remain attached to the calico after felting so the calico can be reused.

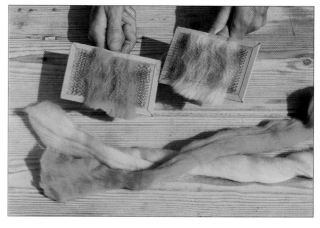

1. Place a small amount of fleece on the teeth of each carder.

Tip

You don't need to buy custom-made carders. Pet combs with wire teeth will do the job and are usually cheaper and more readily available.

Tip

Use a reverse action to clear the carders of excess fibres when changing colours.

2. Gently draw one carder across the other until the fibres are fully combed.

Combed wool fibres. Notice how the two colours have mixed together.

Marbling

On page 24, two different-coloured fibres were used to show how the fibres combine during carding. Mixing colours in this way can be used to create a variegated or marbled effect. This will help you achieve areas of light and dark in the felt, which will give a more painterly effect to your designs and depth to the background.

Marbling can also be done by mixing the fibres by hand. This results in bolder patches of colour than is achieved by the carding method.

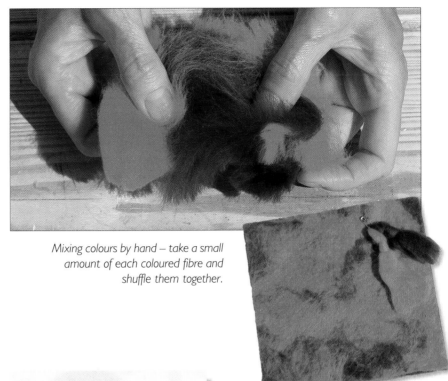

Mixing colours by hand – take a small amount of each coloured fibre and shuffle them together.

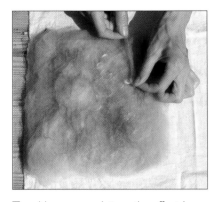

To achieve a more interesting effect, lay out the fibres in the usual way and add silks to the top layer. Wisp over them with fine merino to secure them.

Tip

Some colour combinations work better than others, so choose carefully. We like to mix a really bright shade with a softer shade, such as bright green and pale green.

Hearts made from half-felt and silk strands were inlayed into a piece of marbled felt to create this pretty design.

The finished piece of felt showing the marbling effect and the silks. This is perfect for cutting out shapes such as leaves for inlaying into a picture.

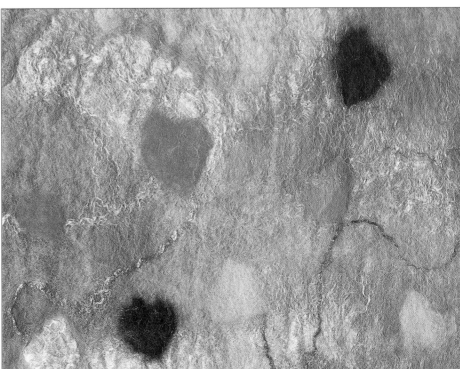

Half-felt

When felt is fairly soft and loose it is known as half-felt or pre-felt. Half-felt can be cut into shapes, placed on a prepared bed of fibres and felted on. This is known as the inlay method and it enables you to create shapes with defined edges within your design.

To make half-felt, the fibres are laid out as shown on pages 17–18, but are felted for a much shorter time (approximately five minutes, or until the fibres are just starting to hold together). If you accidentally felt the half-felt for too long, you can 'rough up' the back with carders to help it attach to the background when using it for inlay.

Saucer felt

Saucer felt is a quick and easy way to make small quantities of half-felt in different colours. You can use it to make small items such as flowers and leaves. It works best for plain pieces of half-felt, as any embellishments such as silks may not attach.

We call it 'saucer' felt because you can literally make it in a saucer or small dish and it takes only a minute or two. Lay out the fibres at right angles to each other, in the same way as shown on page 17. To make larger pieces of half-felt it is best to use the calico and bubble wrap method. Felt the fibres together for a few minutes, or until they have started to lock together.

You can use saucer felt while it is still wet and soapy. Just cut it to shape and drop it on to your prepared bed of fibres.

> **Tip**
>
> Keep a collection of half-felt shapes – reminiscent of childhood 'fuzzy felt' – to use in future projects.

> **You will need**
>
> Merino combed tops in three complementary colours
> Rubber gloves
> Shallow dish
> Jug, soap flakes and hot water
> Balloon whisk
> Towel

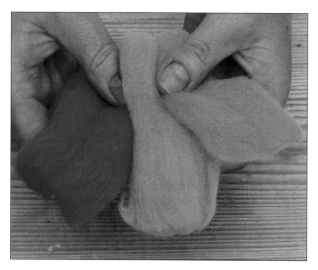

1. Cut three pieces of the combed merino tops (one of each colour) approximately 10cm (4in) long.

2. Place the first piece in a dish with the second piece on top at right angles to the layer below.

Tip

Make a pile of half-felts in different colours for use in future projects. Larger pieces such as these are best made using the calico and bubble wrap method.

3. Place the third layer on top, again at right angles to the layer below.

4. Mix up a soapy solution of hot water and soap flakes in a jug using a balloon whisk.

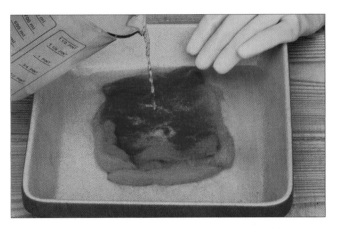

5. Pour the solution over the fibres until they are soaked. Pat gently, wearing rubber gloves, to encourage the fibres to begin to felt.

Tip

Don't over-felt by rubbing the half-felt for too long – the idea is to complete the felting process after it has been transferred to your design.

6. Rub the felt between your hands until the fibres just begin to come together. This usually takes about two minutes, so don't rub for too long.

Complete the half-felt by rinsing it under the tap, holding it gently in your hand, then squeezing the felt in a towel to remove the excess water.

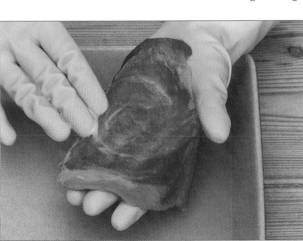

Design

We really enjoy developing ideas and themes, and most of our inspiration is found in nature; flowers, plants, fish and animals make wonderful subjects. A favourite photograph, greetings card or painting is often a good starting point for a design. Look out for simple, strong shapes that will translate well into felt. For example, a stylised rose from the programme of a flower and craft festival that we took part in became the inspiration for our roses design on pages 44–47.

Look around you for ideas, whether they are flowers or trees, tropical fish, a child's paintbox or a field of sheep. You can also combine elements from more than one source to come up with a fresh idea.

This photograph of poppies taken by Shirley's aunt was the starting point for the design of our poppies tea cosy. We were inspired by the strong shapes and colour of the poppy heads. We then did some paintings before starting to work with the felt to give us an idea of how well different colours work together. We use watercolours, but pastels, crayons or felt-tips work just as well.

Often the key to a pleasing design is simplicity. Don't try to incorporate all the elements of a picture but concentrate on a few key details. Our waterlilies design on pages 38–41 uses only four waterlilies and a few irises, which are complemented by the rich textures and glorious colours in the background.

We find it helps to take photographs and make watercolour sketches to crystallise our ideas. We experiment with the colours and the composition and, when we are happy with the design, we make our piece of felt based on that particular theme.

All of the items in this picture are based on the poppies theme — only the colours and the composition have been changed.

Projects

It is hard not to get enthusiastic about making felt. Using just a few simple, natural ingredients you can create a huge array of brightly coloured, beautifully textured items that you can use to adorn your home, or even yourself. We are constantly amazed at the versatility of felt and the way it can be used to make such diverse items as sheer wallhangings, cushion covers, tea cosies and scarves, and even cards and small items such as bookmarks, pincushions and egg cosies.

In all of these projects, with the exception of the alpaca project, we have used merino combed tops, but any kind of wool fibre can be used instead. The emphasis throughout is very much on colour and texture. And finally, feltmaking is addictive – as soon as you have finished one project you will want to start another!

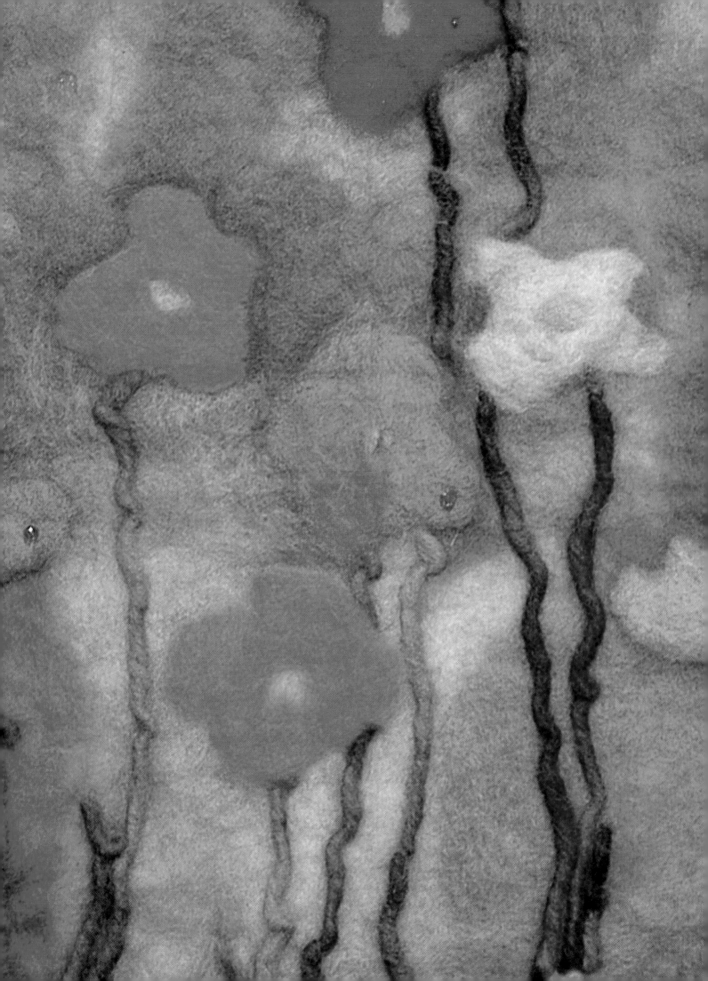

Meadow

This is a lovely project to get you started. It demonstrates the inlay method using half-felt (see pages 26–27) and dip-dyed yarns. One characteristic that makes felt so pleasing to work with is that it does not fray when it is cut. Here, we decided to cut round some of the colourful petals so it looks as though the flowers are spilling over the edge. This gives a more interesting shape to the picture.

We found some lovely multi-coloured dip-dyed yarns to use for stalks, which went well with the variegated background.

Templates for the flowers, three-quarters actual size.

You will need

Washed calico, approximately 60 x 50cm (24 x 20in)

Merino combed tops in cream and small amounts of lemon, two shades of green, turquoise and pale blue for the background

Saucer felt in red, yellow, orange, pink and white for the flower heads

Multi-coloured dip-dyed yarns for the stems

Small pieces of coloured merino or silk strands for the flower centres

Small beads

2B pencil

Metal ruler

Scissors

Dressmaking pins

Needle and thread

Rubber gloves

Large shallow plastic tray

Bubble wrap

Jug, soap flakes and hot water

Vinegar

Towel

Iron

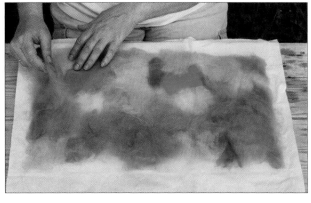

1. Mark out an area 45cm x 25cm (18 x 10in) on the calico in pencil. Lay out the fibres on the calico, following the method described on pages 17–18. Start with two layers of cream, then marble together the lemon, greens, turquoise and pale blue for the third layer.

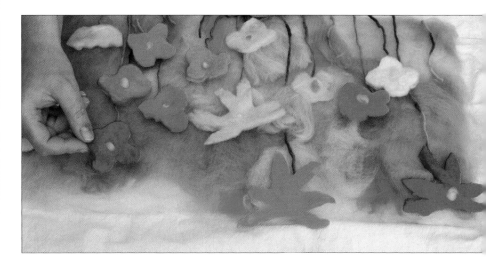

2. Using the templates, cut flower shapes from the half-felt made using the saucer-felt method (see below). Arrange them on the background. Make sure some of the flowers extend a little way beyond the edge of the background. Use dip-dyed yarns for the stems.

For each flower, pin a template to a piece of half-felt, and carefully cut around the flower shape.

To give a centre to a flower, snip a small hole in the middle. Push some silk strands or half-felt through to make the centre.

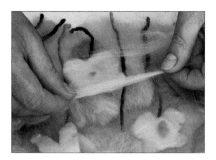

3. Use wisps of merino to cover the stems so they are incorporated into the finished piece.

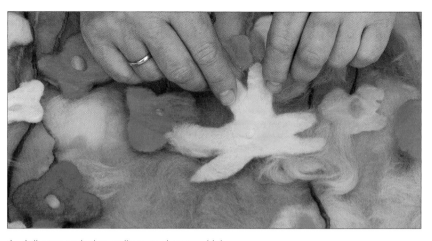

4. Adjust your design until you are happy with it.

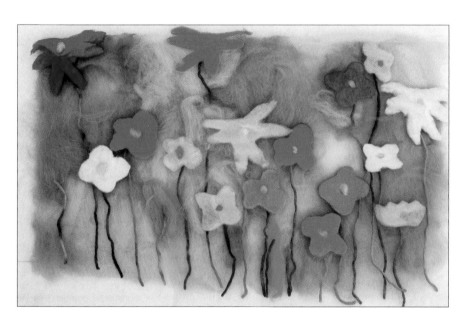

5. You are now ready to start the wet stage of felting. Fold over the calico so that it covers the fibres and stitch it in place to secure the flowers and prevent them from moving around too much (see page 18, steps 12 and 13). Felt in the normal way, as explained on page 19.

6. After felting for about fifteen minutes, check that the fibres have felted properly, and then carefully pull back the calico to reveal the finished piece (see page 20). We love this stage – it's a bit like unwrapping a Christmas present!

7. Rinse the felt thoroughly to remove all traces of soap, and then dry it. Follow the method described on pages 20–21, steps 22–26.

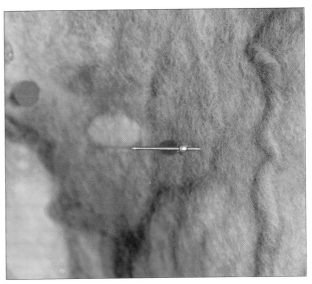

8. After drying your felt you can embellish it by stitching on some beads.

9. Felt does not fray so you can cut back the edges, leaving some of the flowers spilling out of the picture.

This matching tea cosy and egg cosy are based on the meadows design and will really brighten up your breakfast table. They were both made by cutting two matching pieces of felt and stitching them together. You can also make a tea cosy that is seamless (see pages 68–71, lollipop flowers). The bee can be made following the instructions on page 76.

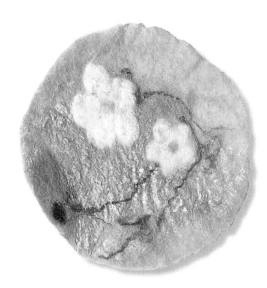

To make this coaster, we inlaid half-felt flowers and used viscose to add sheen. We created the coaster shape by cutting round a saucer pressed on to the wet felt. If the edges are too loose after cutting out, you can re-felt them.

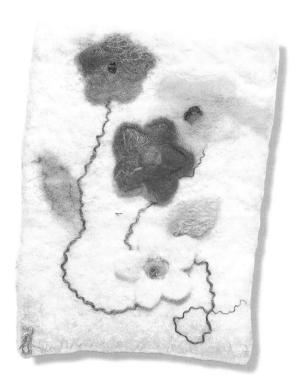

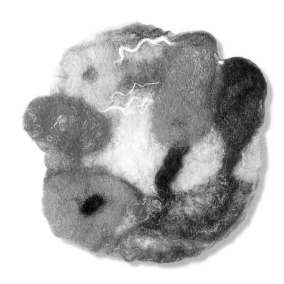

This coaster was inspired by the distinctive tree shapes and larger-than-life foreground flowers typical of the style of Clarice Cliff.

These two panels show how the meadow theme can be applied on a smaller scale, and using different colour combinations. Small pieces like this can be turned into coasters, pincushions and egg cosies (see pages 76–79).

Waterlilies

Claude Monet's impressionist paintings were the starting point for this design. We took some photographs of a lily pond and realised that the distinctive shape of the lilies and lily pads could be effectively re-created in felt. We have used the inlay technique (see page 26) for the details in this wallhanging, and Monet's palette of blues, greens, turquoise, jade and purples gives a jewel-like effect. The silks and decorative yarns are designed to catch the light, giving the impression of shimmering water.

Tip

If you are thinking of making a large wallhanging it is a good idea to test out your ideas by making a smaller piece first.

Templates for the lilies, lily pads and irises, half actual size.

You will need

Washed calico, approximately 80 x 60cm (32 x 24in)

Merino combed tops in shades of blue, purple, turquoise and jade for the background

Turquoise and green mulberry silks

Hand-dyed mohair curls in shades of silver and green

Dip-dyed yarn for the weeds

Half-felts:

Green for the iris stalks

Pinky-red with silks for the waterlilies

Light and dark green with silks for the lily pads

Bright yellow and lemon with silks for the irises

2B pencil

Metal ruler

Scissors

Dressmaking pins

Needle and thread

Rubber gloves

Large shallow plastic tray

Bubble wrap

Jug, soap flakes and hot water

Vinegar

Towel

Iron

1. Draw a rectangle on the right-hand side of the calico measuring 50 x 35cm (20 x 14in) and lay out three layers of merino fibres, marbling together the different shades of blue (see page 25).

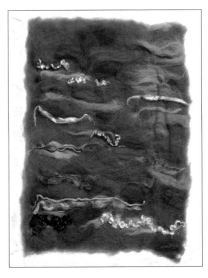

2. On the top layer create areas of interest using mohair curls, mulberry silks and wisps of purple, turquoise and jade merino to simulate the lights and shadows in the water.

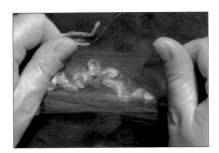

3. Cover any silks or yarns with wisps of merino. This is especially important when using the springy mohair curls to make sure they are anchored securely to the wool fibres.

Tip

To mimic the effect of water, the top layer of fibres should run horizontally, i.e. left to right. So for this three-layer piece of felt, you need to start with fibres running from left to right at layer 1.

4. Use dip-dyed yarn for the weeds. Cut long slivers from green half-felt for the iris stalks and place them on the right-hand side of your design.

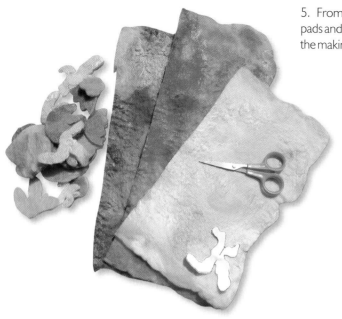

5. From the sheets of pink, green and yellow half-felt, cut out the lilies, lily pads and irises using the templates printed on page 38. We used lots of silks in the making of these half-felts to give depth and shimmer.

> ### Tip
>
> Use a smudge of pink in the top left of the picture to represent a distant lily and give a feeling of perspective.

6. Position the lilies, lily pads and irises.

> ### Tip
>
> If you have a digital camera take a picture of your work before felting it. The camera will often pick up design blunders that the eye does not notice.

7. Make sure you are happy with your composition (there is still time at this stage to change things around) and then felt in the normal way (see pages 16–21).

The completed waterlilies wallhanging.

Above: *These two cushions were made by mounting the felt panel on to velvet – this sumptuous material complements the richness of the design perfectly.*

Opposite: *Felt can be made in a huge range of textures, depending on the method used. This wonderfully delicate, translucent piece of felt was based on a similar design and colour palette to the waterlilies wallhanging, and made following the applied felt method described on page 74.*

Roses

The idea for writing this book came to us after we had participated in a flower and craft festival and discovered that people really seem to like felt! This was our first public event and the inspiration for this project comes from a rose design that was used for the festival programme.

Templates for the roses and leaves, three-quarters actual size.

Tip

If you give an item made from handmade felt as a gift, you can use your inspirational sketches to make matching gift tags. Tie the corner of the tag with a piece of matching dip-dyed yarn or merino.

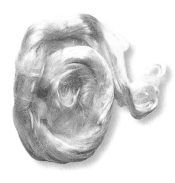

You will need

Washed calico, approximately
45 x 85cm (18 x 34in)

Merino combed tops in lime-lemon, cream, lemon and citrus for the background

A few wisps of dark green fibres for shadows

Mulberry silk tops in cream and lemon-yellow

Dip-dyed yarn in dark greens for stalks

Marbled pink/red, marbled yellows and marbled green half-felt for flowers and leaves

2B pencil

Metal ruler

Scissors

Dressmaking pins

Needle and thread

Rubber gloves

Large shallow plastic tray

Bubble wrap

Jug, soap flakes and hot water

Vinegar

Towel

Iron

Cutting mat and rotary cutter

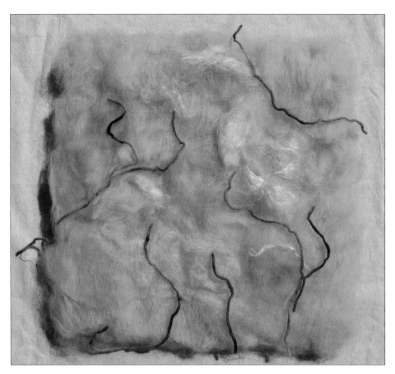

1. Mark out a 38cm (15in) square in pencil on the right-hand side of the calico, making sure there is enough fabric to flap over after you have laid out the fibres. Lay out the fibres following the method described on pages 17–18. Use lime-lemon for the first layer, followed by a mix of lime-lemon, cream and lemon for layers two and three. Add some of the citrus fibres and a few wisps of dark green to the final layer to create areas of brightness and shadow. Add mulberry silk tops in cream and lemon-yellow, wisping over with merino to ensure that they 'felt in', and finally create the stalks pattern using the dip-dyed yarn.

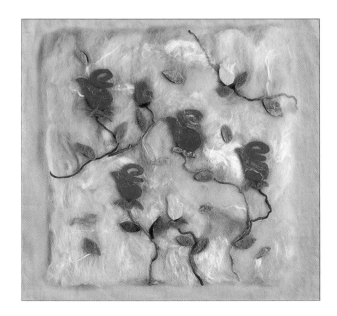

Tip

Try to avoid creating two zones of colour in your design. Here, carefully positioned yellow roses balance out the predominantly pink blooms.

2. Using the templates on page 44, cut out the flower heads in pink/red and yellow and a few green leaves from the half-felt. Start to build up your pattern by placing the roses, rose buds and leaves on the prepared background. Cut small pieces, in a shallow cup shape, from the green half-felt to place underneath the flower heads. Scatter a few extra leaves around if you wish. Felt in the normal way.

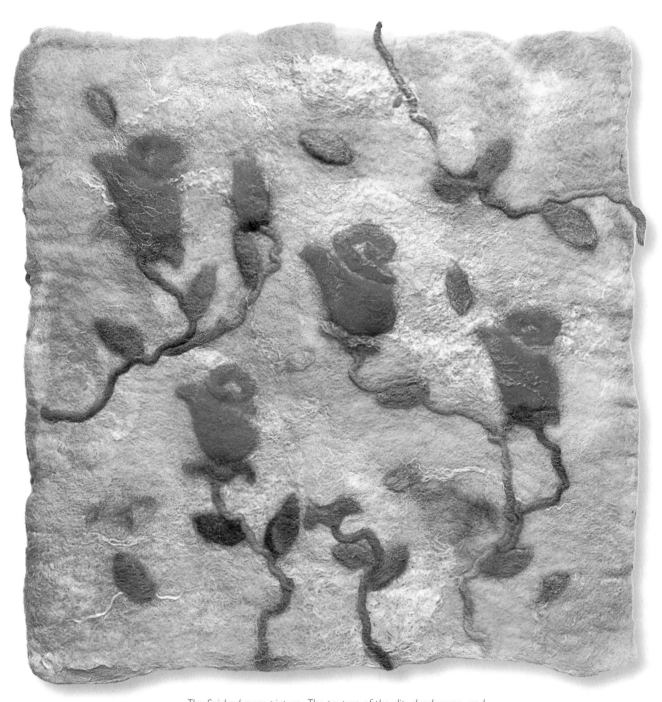

The finished roses picture. The texture of the dip-dyed yarns, and their variegated colours, make them highly effective when used as stalks and stems. The edges of the panel have been cropped and then re-felted, giving them a slightly wavy appearance.

The roses panel works very well as a cushion. Make two, slightly different versions to adorn a plain sofa or chair.

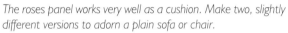

Fibres can be moulded to a particular shape, as in our felt bodice. Merino fibres inlaid with half-felt and silks were laid out flat on calico and felted until the fibres were just beginning to lock together. The whole thing was then wrapped around a tailor's dummy (covered in plastic) and felted using bubble wrap for friction until it shrank to the shape of the dummy. The back of the bodice is secured by six sets of hooks and eyes and three pearl buttons. Button holes were easy to create because felt does not fray.

The straggling yarns add interest to the bottom of the bodice and are the result of a last-minute decision not to snip them off!

Underwater

We chose slightly muted colours for this project but you could ring the changes by using more vibrant colours to create a tropical fish scene.

The fish are cut from half-felt decorated with carefully positioned stripes and spots. It's worth spending a bit of time when laying out the fibres for the half-felt to make sure there are interesting areas from which to cut the fish shapes. Cut out a fish-shaped reverse template to help identify the best areas, and make adjustments to the positioning of spots and stripes as necessary.

Templates for the underwater creatures, three-quarters actual size.

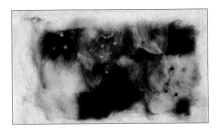

1. Begin by making a piece of half-felt from which to cut the fish shapes. Use lime-lemon for the first layer, followed by two thin layers of cream and black arranged in patches or marbled, depending on the effect you want to create. Add tiny circles of brightly coloured half-felt for the fish markings.

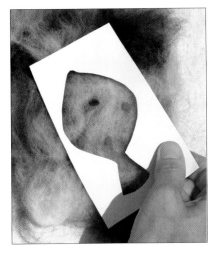

2. Using a fish-shaped reverse template as a guide, make adjustments to the pattern of the spots before felting for about five minutes, or until the fibres just start to hold together.

You will need

Washed calico, approximately 35 x 70cm (14 x 28in)

Merino combed tops in shades of blue, French navy, turquoise, jade and dark green for the background; bobbly decorative yarn for bubbles; dip-dyed yarns for weeds; silks; ramie; mohair curls and dip-dyed roving

Wool fibres in lime-lemon, black and cream to make the half-felt fish shapes; brightly coloured dots of half-felt

Half-felt made from a mix of soft lime, lime, citrus green, bright yellow and lemon for other fish and weeds

Tiny black beads for fish eyes

2B pencil

Metal ruler

Scissors

Dressmaking pins

Needle and thread

Rubber gloves

Large shallow plastic tray

Bubble wrap

Jug, soap flakes and hot water

Vinegar

Towel

Iron

3. Pin the templates on to the half-felt and cut out your fish. Any shapes you do not use, such as the little crab shown here, can be kept for future projects.

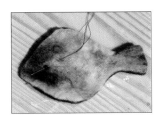

4. Sew on a small black bead for the eye. It is easier to do this at this stage rather than after felting your underwater scene, and the thread will not show.

5. You can cut back the black and cream layer to expose the lime/lemon colour for a fin or tail.

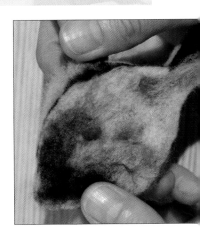

6. Tease out the lime/lemon fibres to emphasise the fin.

7. To make the wallhanging, build the background from a first layer of French navy, a second layer of turquoise and a third layer of marbled blues. Make sure the top layer of fibres runs horizontally to mimic water. Add silks and mohair curls, and fish and weeds cut from the half-felt. Add plenty of silks to make the water really sparkle!

Tip

A pleasing composition is achieved by making sure the fish swim into the picture rather than facing out of it.

8. Add dip-dyed yarns to represent straggly weeds and bobbly yarns for bubbles. Slivers of ramie (the thin white strips in the picture) will crinkle when felted to give a wavy effect.

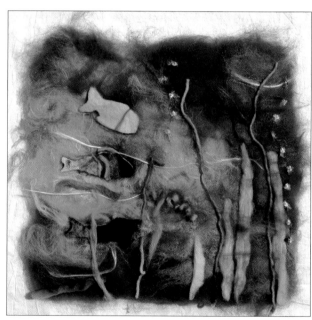

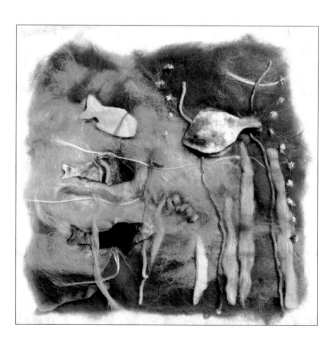

9. The large fish provides a focal point. Position the weeds and bubbles so that it looks as if the fish are swimming through them. Once you are happy with your composition, felt in the normal way (see pages 16–21).

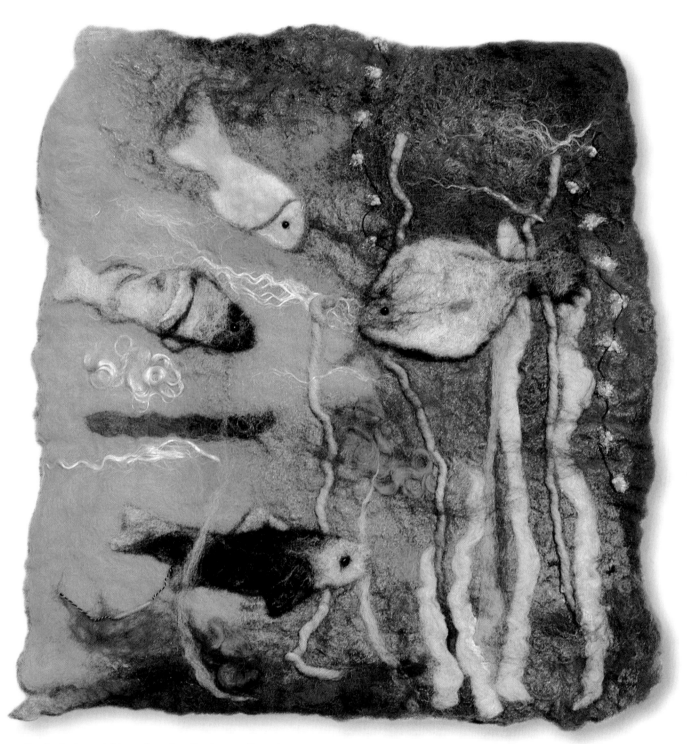

The finished panel. Notice how the silks give sparkle to the water.

sheep

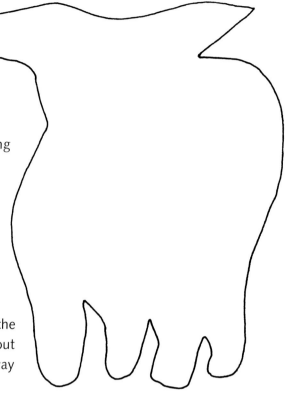

Here we show how to make cut-out sheep in different colours, using Wensleydale curls for an authentic texture.

We attach curtain rings to the back of the sheep and hang them on a twisted willow branch. This makes a wonderful centrepiece, perhaps for a craft fair display or an Easter decoration. Add a string of tiny fairylights for a truly magical effect.

We like this project because no two sheep ever come out the same. The sheep shapes are arranged on a bed of fibres, using a reverse template (as in the fish project) to check positioning.

You can make several sheep in one go, and after felting the sheep are 'released' from the background by cutting them out with sharp scissors. All are slightly different because of the way the fibres move during felting, and the tilt of the head or 'springiness' of the legs gives each one its own character.

Template for the sheep, three-quarters actual size, and a separate template for its head (also three-quarters actual size).

You will need

Washed calico, approximately
35 x 70cm (14 x 28in)

Merino combed tops in lime-lemon
and cream for the background

Merino combed tops in shades of
pink and yellow for the sheep

Wensleydale curls

Black or brown half-felt for legs
and heads

2B pencil

Metal ruler

Scissors

Dressmaking pins

Needle and thread

Rubber gloves

Large shallow plastic tray

Bubble wrap

Jug, soap flakes and hot water

Vinegar

Towel

Iron

Carders

Curtain rings

To make four sheep in one go, prepare a 30cm (12in) square bed of fibres using three layers of merino (we used lime-lemon for the first layer, followed by two layers of cream). Remember to alternate the direction of each layer of fibres as usual.

Cut heads from the brown or black half-felt using the template provided on page 52. To make the legs, cut narrow rectangles – you don't need to be too precise about this.

Roughly position the heads and legs. Allow an area covering about a quarter of the laid-out fibres for each sheep.

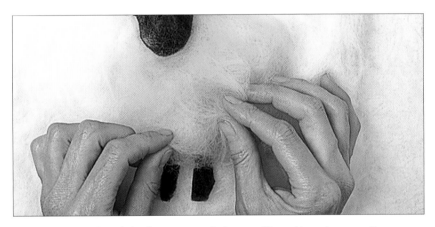

1. To make the sheep's bodies, use a carded mass of fibres (there is no need to worry about layers). Choose whatever colours you prefer. We used yellows and pinks, but natural colours look beautiful too.

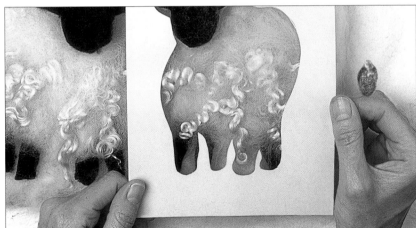

2. Check the position of the head and legs using the sheep-shaped reverse template. Make sure the tops of the legs are tucked under the fluffy fibres. The head should rest on top of the fibres.

Tip

Tease out some of the Wensleydale curls so they hang over the edge of your sheep shape.

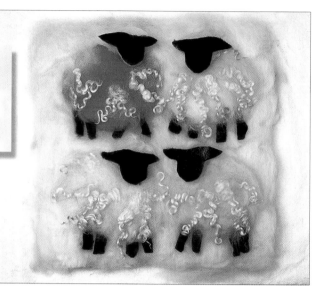

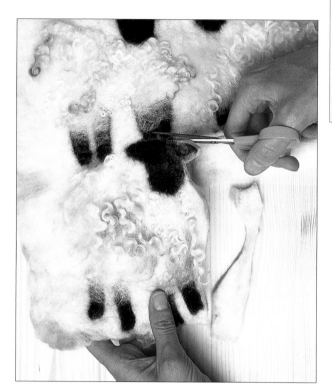

3. Add masses of Wensleydale curls and, as usual, wisp over with some merino strands to make sure they remain attached. Cover the fibres with the calico, stitch around the edges and felt for about fifteen minutes or until felted. Use the method described on page 19.

4. Release the sheep from the background, being careful not to snip through any overhanging Wensleydale curls. If the edges seem too loose they can be re-felted.

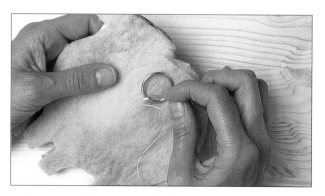

5. Sew a curtain ring on the back of each sheep.

The sheep are a great 'make' for selling at craft fairs. You can mass produce them by laying out a much bigger background layer of fibres and cramming the sheep shapes on.

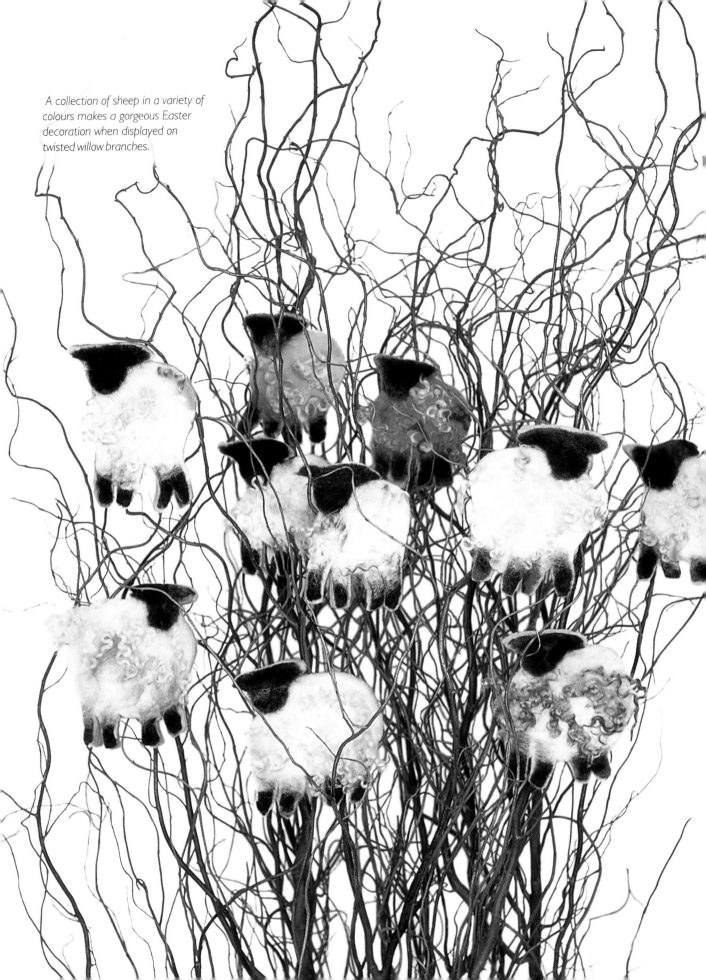

A collection of sheep in a variety of colours makes a gorgeous Easter decoration when displayed on twisted willow branches.

Alpaca

Alpaca fleece is comparable to cashmere and known for its fineness, light weight and lustre – all characteristics that make it ideal for feltmaking. The fibres are hairier than merino, and may take a little longer to felt, but the result is lovely and soft.

Our alpaca wallhanging was inspired by a visit to a local alpaca farm where we watched these delightful creatures grazing in a meadow – and were even lucky enough to see a baby alpaca (cria) being born.

Templates for the alpacas and flowers, half actual size.

1. Lay out a bed of fibres on the calico measuring 35 x 50cm (14 x 20in). The first two layers are cream. The top layer of fibres is divided into two areas. For the upper half, marble together the darker greens to resemble the forest, and for the lower half use yellows and lighter greens for the meadow. Add pale yellow and dark green silks for a hint of reflected sunlight.

You will need

Washed calico, approximately 76 x 56cm (30 x 22in)

Alpaca fibres in cream, shades of dark green for the forest, and yellows and lighter greens for the meadow

Thick brown yarn or roving for tree trunks

Mohair curls in cream for the alpacas' tails, and green for bushes and undergrowth

Half-felt in pale pink, pale yellow and white for the flowers

Pale yellow and dark green silks

Natural cream and light brown alpaca fibres for the alpacas

Black thread for eyes

Beads for decoration

2B pencil

Metal ruler

Scissors

Dressmaking pins

Needle and thread

Carders

Rubber gloves

Large shallow plastic tray

Bubble wrap

Jug, soap flakes and hot water

Vinegar

Towel

Iron

2. In the forest area, use short lengths of thickish brown yarns or roving tucked behind the top layer of green fibres to look like tree trunks in the distance. Add small patches of fibres of various shades of green, perhaps adding some green mohair curls, to resemble bushes and undergrowth. Cut out the flower shapes using the template on page 56 (to make the centres of the flowers, see page 33). Place the cut-out flower shapes in the meadow area using yellow and green silks for stems.

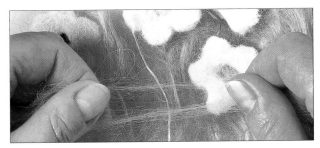

3. Cover the silk stems with wisps of merino to secure them.

4. For the alpacas, make a piece of half-felt from a mixture of cream and light brown fibres. (We used natural alpaca fibres but you can also use merino.) Use the templates to cut out the shapes from the half-felt. Ensure that your alpacas have some interesting markings by using a reverse template, as in the fish project on page 49.

5. Complete the alpacas by using black thread for their eyes and cream mohair curls for their tails, and place them on the bed of fibres. The heads should be against the darker forest background so that they stand out clearly. Felt your design in the normal way (see pages 16–21).

The finished picture. Note the silks shimmering in the forest.

The panel can be made into a fabulous cushion cover, like the one above. Tiny glinting beads have been added for extra sparkle! Smaller pieces based on the same design can be made into pincushions (see page 77). In the top picture, the alpaca has been felted on to the background using the inlay method; in the bottom picture it has been sewn on after felting.

This cushion, egg cosy and wallhanging show how natural, undyed alpaca fleece can be used to create more subtle effects. Instructions for making a similar cushion using dyed wool fibres are given on page 22.

Apples and squares

Apples and pears are strong, attractive shapes for use in feltmaking designs. We chose apples for our piece but you could use pears instead. The bright reds, yellows and greens enhance the freshness and simplicity of the design.

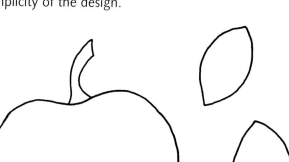

Templates for apples and leaves, three-quarters actual size.

1. Use the cutting mat and cutter to cut out 24 squares of half-felt, each measuring 5cm (2in), for the mosaic border. Use a metal ruler, and always cut away from you. You will need 24 squares altogether. Any left-over squares can be kept for future projects.

You will need

Washed calico, approximately 45 x 60cm (18 x 24in)

Merino combed tops in cream, lemon and bright yellow for the background

Five A4-size pieces of half-felt in pink, lime green, soft lime, marbled reds and marbled yellows for mosaic squares, apples and leaves

Cream, yellow and white tussah silks

Green or brown roving for apple stalks

2B pencil

Metal ruler

Scissors

Dressmaking pins

Needle and thread

Carders

Rubber gloves

Large shallow plastic tray

Bubble wrap

Jug, soap flakes and hot water

Vinegar

Towel

Iron

Cutting mat and rotary cutter

2. Make the background, starting with a layer of cream then marbling the two yellows (see page 25) for the second and third layers. It should measure 46 x 26cm (18 x 10in). Add plenty of cream and yellow silks to the background before adding the mosaic square border.

3. Complete the mosaic edges, then cut out the apples and leaves using the templates and place them on the background. We found that a row of three apples makes a pleasing composition. Use green or brown roving for the stalks. Add a highlight to each apple using a strand of white silk. This produces a three-dimensional effect and gives the picture depth. Secure the silks with wisps of merino. When you are happy with your composition, felt it in the normal way (see pages 16–21).

Tip

If we are not happy with a finished piece we sometimes cut it up and use the fragments to make items such as cards and pincushions. This is an example of the way felt can be recycled in interesting ways.

The finished piece could be used as a place mat, or the centre panel for a rectangular cushion. Use pears instead of apples for an interesting variation.

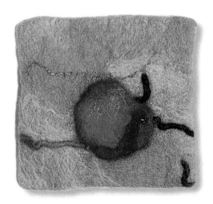

Apples and pears coasters

These colourful coasters would work very well with a set of apples and squares place mats. They were created by laying out a small square of fibres and adding a stalk and leaves cut from half-felt. The fibres were then felted and the apple and pear shapes were cut out. You could make several fruits on one piece of felt, as in the sheep project (page 53).

This coaster is one of a set made by cutting down a larger piece of felt.

This tea cosy was made using the method shown on page 69. It has a pears design on one side and apples on the other. The cushion (below) was made in a similar way to the place mat, but instead of using half-felt squares for the edge we laid on coloured merino fibres. The fruity felt scarf (opposite) in jewel-like colours is lined with satin.

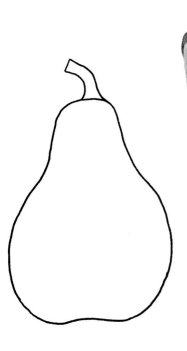

Template for the pear, three-quarters actual size.

Felted stones

Felt can be shaped around solid objects such as stones without the need for seams. The result is an intriguing object that people instinctively want to touch and, like the ship in the bottle technique, everyone wants to know how it's done!

Lay out three layers of fibres to cover an area roughly four times the size of your stone. Be generous – you can always get rid of unwanted fibres later on (you do not need to place the stone under the fibres at this stage). We used burgundy, rose and bright pink mixed together for the felt. Gold tussah silk was added to the top layer to resemble veins in marble.

You will need

Stones

A piece of calico big enough to wrap around your stones

Merino combed tops in burgundy, rose and bright pink

Gold tussah silk

Rubber gloves

Large shallow plastic tray

Bubble wrap

Jug, soap flakes and hot water

Look out for cobbles in different shapes and sizes to make the felted stones. The gold tussah silk (second left) is used to achieve the marbled effect.

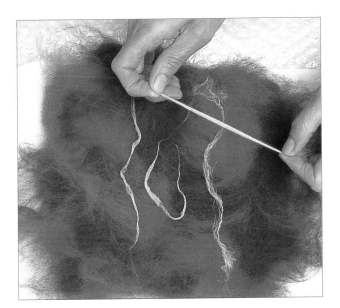

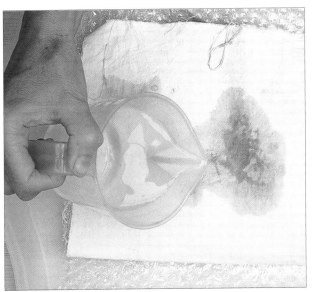

1. Marble together the background colours, then add slivers of gold silk to resemble veins. Before positioning the silks, wet them slightly by dipping your fingers into some warm water. This will make the silks easier to work with. Cover the silks with a few wisps of merino to secure them.

2. Felt the fibres for a minute or two to make them more manageable, before adding the stone. Concentrate on the area in the centre of the fibres only. Try to keep the edges dry. Cover the fibres with the calico, pour on some hot water and add a few soap flakes. If you work the fibres too much at this stage you will not be able to achieve a neat join around the back of the stone.

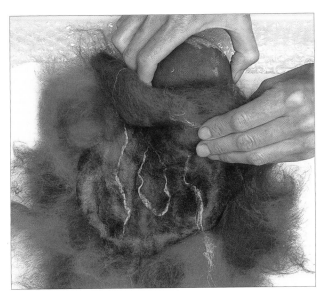

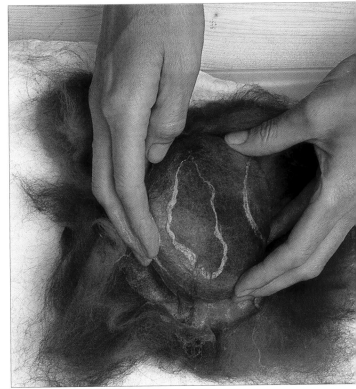

3. Peel back the calico and slip the stone underneath the wetted area of fibres.

4. Tuck the fibres around the edges of the stone. Don't worry about the back at this stage.

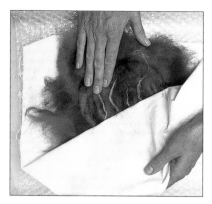

5. Cover the stone and the fibres with the calico, add more water and soap flakes if necessary and felt for a few more minutes so that the fibres start to take the shape of the stone.

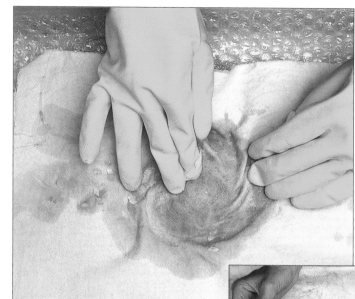

6. Rub the top and sides, following the contours of the stone.

7. Remove the stone from the calico, turn it over and break off the excess fibres.

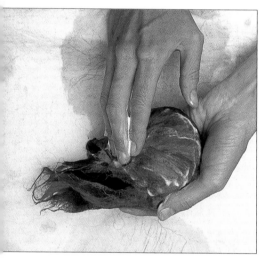

8. Leave enough fibres so that you can 'dovetail' them together to form a neat join at the back of the stone. This is the tricky bit, and you may need a few practices to get it right. If you leave too many fibres the join will be bulky, too few and the felt will be too thin. You can adjust the silks at this stage to make sure they wrap neatly around the stone.

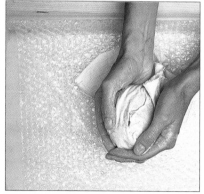

9. Wrap the stone in calico again and continue felting to stabilise the fibres around it. You can use bubble wrap to create some extra friction if necessary.

10. Remove the calico and continue to felt the stone by turning it over and over in your bare hands, adding a few more soap flakes to make it nice and slippery. The longer you do this, the firmer the felt will be. Rinse thoroughly.

Felted stones make an intriguing gift. You can use them as paperweights or doorstops – or group them together as an artistic arrangement.

Lollipop flowers

Felt is a great insulator, and this tea cosy really does keep the tea hot. It is also washable. The fibres are folded around a resist material – in this case thick bubble wrap – and felted so there are no seams.

The stylised lollipop-shaped flowers were inspired by an unusual Clarice Cliff design called Latona Flowerheads that we found on the internet. The vibrant orange, blue and green shapes with black centres make a striking contrast to the cream-coloured background.

Templates for the tea cosy pattern, half actual size.

Template for the tea cosy. This needs to be enlarged by 350 per cent, or until the base edge measures approximately 30cm (12in).

Cut a tea cosy shape from the resist material (thick bubble wrap/polystyrene) using your paper template. The resist tea cosy shape will be sandwiched between the fibres to prevent the two sides of the tea cosy from felting together.

You will need

Washed calico, approximately 50 x 70cm (20 x 28in)

Resist material (thick bubble wrap or thin polystyrene)

Merino combed tops in cream and lime-lemon for the background

Three pieces of half-felt (approximately 20cm or 8in square) in marbled blues, marbled greens and orange (all with added silks)

Small amount of black and cream half-felt for flower centres

2B pencil

Metal ruler

Scissors

Dressmaking pins

Carders

Rubber gloves

Large shallow plastic tray

Bubble wrap

Jug, soap flakes and hot water

Vinegar

Water sprayer

Towel

Iron

Cutting mat and rotary cutter

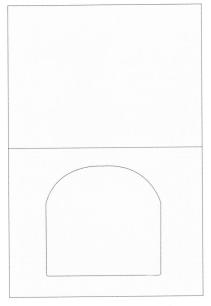

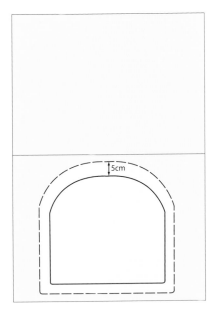

Start by marking out the tea cosy shape in pencil on the calico, again using your paper template. Use the calico vertically, as shown in the diagram, so there is enough material to flap over from the top (rounded edge) to the bottom (straight edge) of the tea cosy.

Place the first layer of fibres (cream) on the calico. The fibres should radiate beyond the area marked out by at least 5cm (2in) because you will be folding them up around the resist when you start to create Side 2 of the tea cosy. Use cream for the next layer, then lime-lemon. Alternate the direction of the fibres for each layer as usual.

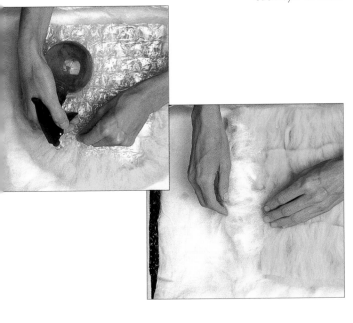

1. After laying out three layers of fibres, place the resist shape on top. Start to fold the fibres towards you, layer by layer, around the resist, using a water spray to make them more pliable. If you have chosen the same colour scheme as shown here, the first layer to be folded over will be the lime-lemon fibres. Do not fold over the fibres along the straight edge of the tea cosy.

2. When you have folded over the first layer of fibres from Side 1, fill in the gaps with more lime-lemon. Make sure that the fibres on Side 2 are running in the same direction as their counterparts on the other side.

3. Continue to build your tea cosy by folding the fibres over from Side 1, layer by layer, and filling the gaps. The second and third layers of Side 2 will be cream merino, matching the fibres on the other side.

4. You can now add decorations cut from the orange, green and blue half-felt, using circles of black and cream for the centre of the flowers.

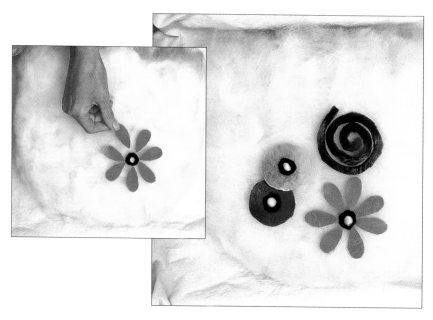

Tip

Use pins to secure the calico, rather than stitches, because they are quicker to remove. You may need to pull back the calico when the fibres are still quite loose to check the curved edges and make any necessary adjustments.

5. When you have decorated one side of the tea cosy, carefully turn the whole thing over and decorate Side 2, with either the same pattern or perhaps just a simplified detail.

6. Cover the fibres with calico and secure with pins before felting in the usual way (see page 19).

Tip

To make the spiral shape, cut a circle of half-felt and cut into it, in a spiral motion, until you reach the centre. Trim back some of the edges to define the shape.

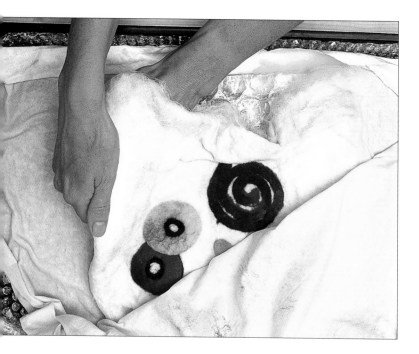

7. When the fibres have started to lock together you should be able to push your hand inside the tea cosy from the bottom (straight edge) as the resist will have created a barrier between the fibres. Put the edge of one hand inside and work the outside of the tea cosy with your other hand to shape the curves. You can remove the resist material when the fibres are still fairly loose but be careful not to let the inside surfaces of the tea cosy start felting together.

8. When the fibres are fully felted, rinse the tea cosy thoroughly, roll in a towel to dry, then press with a warm iron. Add a few drops of vinegar to the final rinse to remove any remaining traces of soap.

9. Trim the lower edge of the tea cosy, turn it in and hem it. You can also line the tea cosy with a matching or toning silky material to make it into a special gift.

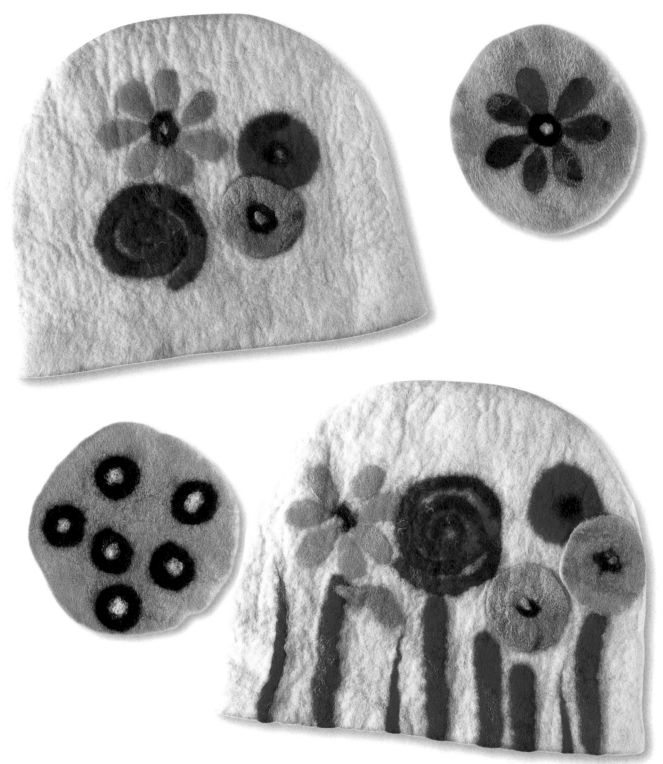

The finished tea cosy is shown top left, and a variation on the design is shown bottom right. You could also make some mats to match, perhaps picking up on elements of the design such as the flower heads.

Paintbox

I n this project we use a different technique known as applied felting. Applied felt is made by arranging cobweb-thin layers of fibres on a lightweight diaphanous material (a 'ground') such as muslin or organza. During felting, the fibres attach to the ground as well as to themselves. The ground lends a little weight to the felt, and makes it a wonderful fabric for draping across a window or using as a wallhanging.

It is also possible to make a similar piece without using a ground. This is known as cobweb felt, but it is rather fragile for a hanging.

This design is based on a simple watercolour paintbox. We used a wide range of toning and complementary colours, but a more limited palette is just as effective.

We recommend you try this project when you have gained a little experience in using and handling the fibres.

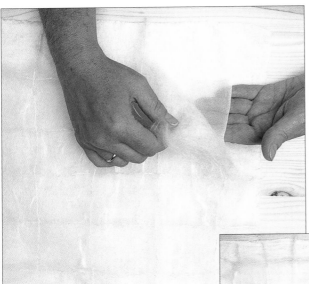

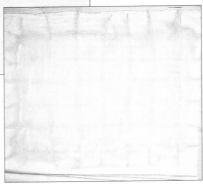

1. Lay the organza on the right-hand side of the calico. Cover the organza with a fine layer of the cream merino fibres. Create a second thin layer with the fibres running in the opposite direction and a third layer with the fibres going in the same direction as the first. There should be no spaces or holes in the fibres.

2. Cut lengths of mohair yarn and lay them out to create a grid of squares, four squares down and six squares across, on top of the fine bed of fibres. Try to make the squares even. You can use a ruler if this helps. You will be putting the coloured squares in this grid.

You will need

Washed calico, approximately 80 x 60cm (32 x 24in)

White organza, 35 x 50cm (14 x 20in)

Cream merino combed tops for the background

24 squares, 4 x 4cm (1½ x 1½in), cut from merino combed tops in a range of colours

Approximately 5m (16½ft) cream mohair yarn

2B pencil

Metal ruler

Scissors

Dressmaking pins

Needle and thread

Carders

Rubber gloves

Large shallow plastic tray

Bubble wrap

Jug, soap flakes and hot water

Balloon whisk

Vinegar

Towel

Iron

Tip

Cut the mohair yarn slightly longer than the organza. You can always trim the ends down to size after felting, or leave them slightly overlapping the edges of the organza as we have done.

3. Carefully place the coloured squares you have cut in the grid so it resembles a paintbox. Keep the squares as even as possible.

When you have placed all the pieces, flap the calico over as usual. Organza is a rather slippery material, so pin and then tack through the calico all over so the squares are secured. Remove the pins after tacking.

To felt the piece, follow the instructions on the next page.

Applied felting

The technique for applied felting is different from normal felting. The fibres attach to the organza by migrating through, and felting takes very little time as only small quantities of fibres are involved. To prevent the fibres and the organza felting to each other immediately, use lukewarm water instead of hot, and a very gentle rubbing action.

1. Mix up a jug of lukewarm soapy water using a balloon whisk and pour it all over, completely soaking the piece. Start with the piece design-side down in the tray so you soap the reverse side first.
2. Press down all over the calico to ensure the entire parcel is soaked.
3. Rub gently for about five minutes.
4. Flip the piece over and rub it with a circular motion on the front side – you can use more pressure now.
5. After another five or ten minutes, untack and lift a corner of the calico to see if the merino fibres have felted through the organza.
6. If so, gently peel back the calico. Remember that the fibres were applied very thinly, so hold them down securely when removing the calico. If the fibres are still very loose, re-cover with the calico and continue felting for a few more minutes.
7. Rinse as usual, adding a few drops of vinegar to the final rinse.

When dry, any squares that have failed to attach to the organza can be secured using invisible stitching.

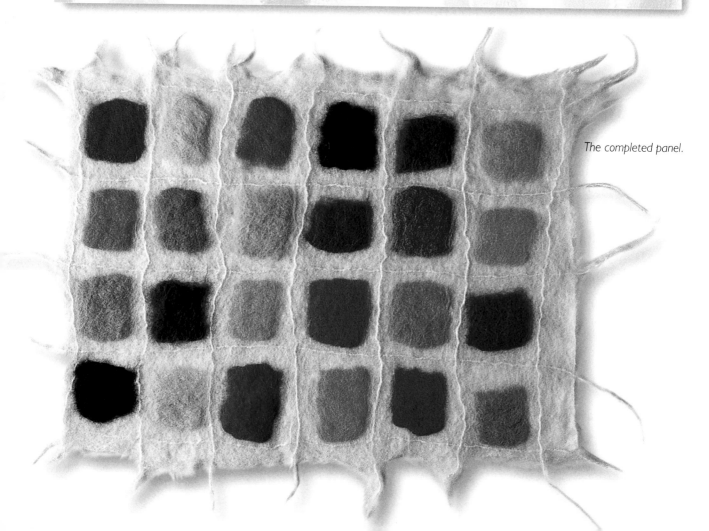

The completed panel.

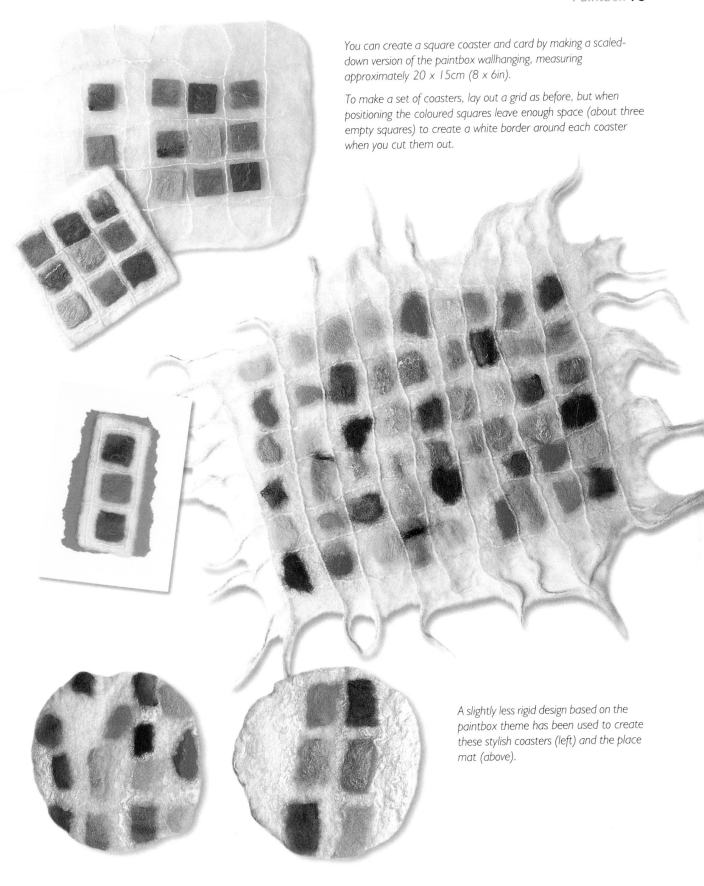

You can create a square coaster and card by making a scaled-down version of the paintbox wallhanging, measuring approximately 20 x 15cm (8 x 6in).

To make a set of coasters, lay out a grid as before, but when positioning the coloured squares leave enough space (about three empty squares) to create a white border around each coaster when you cut them out.

A slightly less rigid design based on the paintbox theme has been used to create these stylish coasters (left) and the place mat (above).

Bees

Bees are great fun to use in your felt designs, and are very easy to make. Begin by making a piece of thick half-felt (five or six layers) using alternate layers of yellow and black-brown. When you cut through this half-felt there will be a stripey cross-section which can be used to make the bees.

Cut a thin strip of the half-felt and turn it so that the stripey part is facing up. Cut an oval shape with slightly blunted ends to make your bee. Use crescent shapes cut from thin scraps of cream or yellow half-felt for the wings.

Sew on a little black bead for the eye, and leave thread dangling for the legs before placing your half-felt bee on to the bed of fibres.

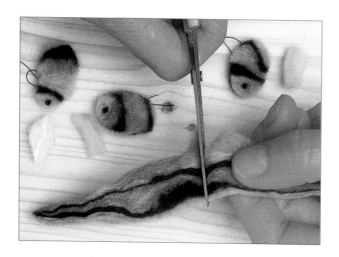

This coaster is made using three fine layers of merino with the pattern inlaid on top. We used a larger-than-life bee here and the flower shapes were cut from scraps left over from the waterlilies wallhanging. Cut the coaster to the shape required after felting. A small round dish or saucer can be used as a template for this. Finish off the edges by re-felting them after cutting.

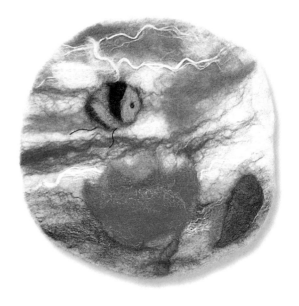

Pincushions

You can make several pincushions in one go by making a piece of patterned felt large enough to cut into, for example, four squares or rectangles.

Cut a square or rectangle of felt and a matching-sized piece of the backing material. We backed our pincushions with cream cotton velvet (using a 'lucky find' set of old curtains bought from a charity shop) but you could use felt for both sides.

Pin the two pieces of fabric together, face to face, and machine stitch three sides (if you have made a rectangular pincushion, leave one of the shorter sides open).

Turn the whole thing right way out. Stuff the pincushion with kapok, or preferably carded merino fibres, before sewing up the remaining side by hand.

You could also fill your pincushion with sand, which will make the finished item pleasingly weighty and – so we are told – will help to keep your pins rust-free and sharp!

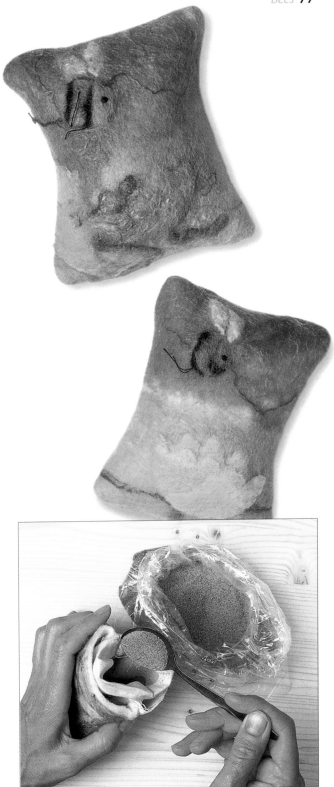

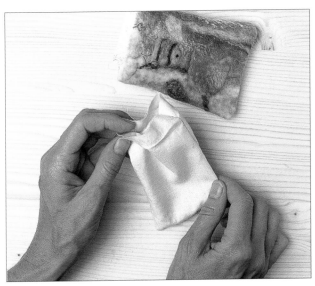

1. If filling with sand, you will need to make an inner bag to contain it, otherwise it will seep out through the felt. Use a close-weave fabric to make a bag that is slightly smaller than your pincushion. Sew up three sides of the bag and leave one side open (if you have made a rectangular pincushion, leave one of the shorter sides open as before). Slip the empty 'sand bag' into the outer pincushion bag (it is easier to do it this way, rather than trying to insert a full bag).

2. Fill the inner bag with dry sand and then sew up the top edge carefully so that the sand cannot leak out. Sew up the outer pincushion to finish off.

Mini makes

Felt does not have to be made on a grand scale – here are some ideas for turning your felt into small items that make excellent gifts for friends and relatives.

If you are making cards, use fine, lightweight pieces of felt or applied felt (see page 74) and mount them on tissue paper. We tear the tissue rather than cutting it to give a softer edge that matches the texture of the felt. Tissue paper has a grain that means it tears more easily in one direction than the other – make the longer edge the one that you tear along the grain rather than against it, as this creates a neater edge.

These cards and gift tag were based on the underwater theme (see page 48). They were given a watercolour background, and embellished with tiny shells and silk yarns to create fronds of seaweed.

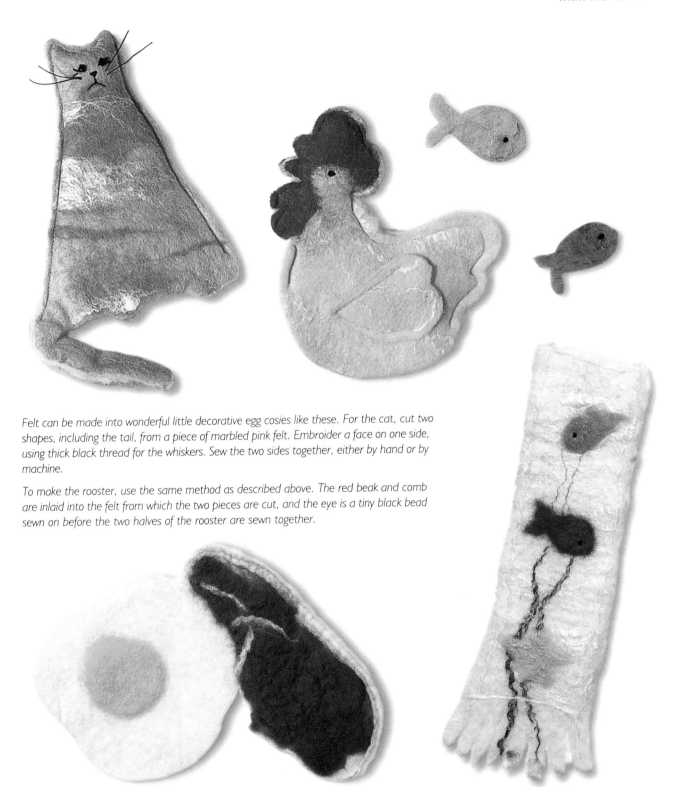

Felt can be made into wonderful little decorative egg cosies like these. For the cat, cut two shapes, including the tail, from a piece of marbled pink felt. Embroider a face on one side, using thick black thread for the whiskers. Sew the two sides together, either by hand or by machine.

To make the rooster, use the same method as described above. The red beak and comb are inlaid into the felt from which the two pieces are cut, and the eye is a tiny black bead sewn on before the two halves of the rooster are sewn together.

This quirky egg and bacon mat was made in one piece, inlaying a yellow circle of half-felt for the egg yolk and silk for the strands of fat in the bacon. Fried egg shapes on their own also work well as coasters.

Tropical-coloured half-felt fish inlayed on white felt have been used to create this colourful bookmark.

Index

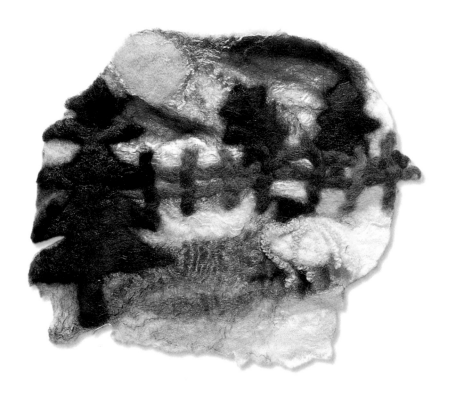